VOODOO

The Secrets of Voodoo from Beginner to Expert

Everything You Need to Know about Voodoo Religion, Rituals, and Casting Spells

by Issendai Bechau

Table of Contents

Introduction 1

Chapter 1: Getting to Know the Essence of Voodoo
.... 7

Chapter 2: Understanding the Nature of Voodoo
Practice 13

Chapter 3: Preparing Yourself for Spells and Rituals
.... 21

Chapter 4: Understanding and Using Voodoo Oils
.... 27

Chapter 5: Understanding and Using Voodoo
Candles and Powders 37

Chapter 6: Learning the Basic Voodoo Spells 49

Chapter 7: Advanced Spells for Protection 65

Chapter 8: Advanced Spells for Revenge 75

Chapter 9: Advanced Spells for Love 83

Chapter 10: Advanced Spells for Healing 95

Chapter 11: Other Useful Spells 101

Conclusion 111

Introduction

While I'm sure that you have *heard* of Voodoo before, and may even think you have an inkling as to what all it entails — don't be so sure about that. Despite Hollywood's best efforts to portray Voodoo as another second-act plot-twist freak show of spirituality, in reality it's been a hallowed religion close to the roots and hearts of millions of global citizens for more years than can be accurately traced back in recorded history.

Voodoo in its current form is the syncretic amalgamation of several West and Central African tribalistic religio-spiritual ways of life, essentially concerned with the positive balance in energies and healing of the world, which took on Christian mantles after the forced conversion of displaced slaves by French rulers on the island of Haiti. From there on, the African-Caribbean immigration to the United States led to further forms developing their own styles in Louisiana, and more specifically in New Orleans. More on that in subsequent chapters, but essentially, Voodoo is a massive, dynamic, ever-growing religion deeply rooted in mystic lifestyles which were already ancient back when Christianity was a fledgling just starting to spread its wings.

Moreover, while Voodoo may seem overly simplified in many sources, its actions and rituals have histories of *exact* reproduction dating back millennia, with significances deeper than can be entirely conveyed in a single book. Therefore, for the uninitiated interested in joining the ranks of modern-day Vodouisants, herein I've compiled the mere essence of decades worth of experiences in order to offer you the an introductory glimpse into the world of Voodoo.

So, are you ready to launch yourself into this unparalleled life which reflects the very *soul* of an entire race of people on this planet? Are you ready to learn the very basics of rituals and spells which would allow you to peek into the spirit world and take your destiny into your very own hands? Well what are you waiting for? Let's get started!

© Copyright 2016 by Miafn LLC - All rights reserved.

This document is geared towards providing reliable information in regards to the topic and issue covered. The publication is sold with the idea that the publisher is not required to render accounting, officially permitted, or otherwise, qualified services. If advice is necessary, legal or professional, a practiced individual in the profession should be ordered.

- From a Declaration of Principles which was accepted and approved equally by a Committee of the American Bar Association and a Committee of Publishers and Associations.

In no way is it legal to reproduce, duplicate, or transmit any part of this document in either electronic means or in printed format. Recording of this publication is strictly prohibited and any storage of this document is not allowed unless with written permission from the publisher. All rights reserved.

The information provided herein is stated to be truthful and consistent, in that any liability, in terms of inattention or otherwise, by any usage or abuse of any policies, processes, or directions contained within is solely and completely the responsibility of the recipient reader. Under no circumstances will any legal responsibility or blame be held against the publisher for any reparation, damages, or monetary loss due to the information herein, either directly or indirectly.

Respective authors own all copyrights not held by the publisher.

The information herein is offered for informational purposes solely, and is universal as so. The presentation of the information is without contract or any type of guarantee assurance.

The trademarks that are used are without any consent, and the publication of the trademark is without permission or backing by the trademark owner. All trademarks and brands within this book are for clarifying purposes only and are the owned by the owners themselves, not affiliated with this document.

Chapter 1: Getting to Know the Essence of Voodoo

Voodoo is the modern-day version of a Haitian religion called Vodou, which was developed under the mantle of French slavery by African-Caribbean slaves working on island plantations. However, it must not be overlooked that whether during its time in "Hispaniola" or after it entered America, it also picked up some Native-American practices and systems of belief within its folds (most notably Arawakian systems of belief). At its very heart, that's a fact of tremendous relevance—that Voodoo originated from a space where adopting Christianity as their religion was the only way to survive for tribes from Central and Western Africa who may have had diverse practices and rituals, but which originated from the same neighborhood of bodies of religious thought. When such people met other mystic spirituals, such as the Native Americans, growing communication within common spaces of living also led to the syncretic assimilation of their beliefs since many Native-American spiritual systems resonated with African spirituality.

Therefore, as Vodou developed into its current form, it encompassed the root essence of African spirituality and some measures of Native American belief systems as well as that of Roman Catholicism, since they needed to publicly espouse Christianity while inserting their own practices into Christian ways, which would allow their traditional beliefs to survive. However, although the root of Catholicism's spiritual seed lay in indoctrination and the force of religious text over the lives of its followers, the same in African spirituality lay in the perception and devotion to the order of the universe, the healing of energies by overbalancing positive forces, and the nature of the spirit or soul which led to spirit possession.

Although Voodoo is a deeply personalized religion, given its esoteric and mystical origins spanning millennia, if one is to try and figure out the most important of its teachings to its practitioners, it's this—there is a definite order through which the world functions, and knowing one's place and respecting it within that order will bring immense positivity and wholesomeness, not only to the practitioner but to the system itself. Now, this shouldn't be misunderstood as becoming a mindless zombie to the system—another myth attributed to Vodouisant Bokors, or the closest thing the religion can have to chaotic or negative sorcerers at the very fringes of Voodoo society. Instead, perceiving and respecting the system is similar to having respect for the forces above you in the order of things, even if you may not see eye to eye and communicate as such.

Within daily life and practice as an example, Voodoo is in itself a complete way of life instead of just a practicable religion, allowing elders to speak before you render your opinion on a topic on which they may have greater experience in life is a reflection of the essence of the religion. Again, don't equate this to the simple "respect your elders" adage, but rather a deep binding sense of order within the way social interactions are constructed and viewed through Voodoo—the "elders" of "tribes", even in modern day life, *must* speak before the younger ones on any matters under discussion because they've spent more time on this planet, and so have facets of knowledge or perspectives that youngsters lack. The same goes for the priestly order, with initiated higher ups having the first say than their lower counterparts. If the juniors disagree with their seniors, they will get their chance to respectfully assert said opinion once the seniors have finished speaking. Therefore, understanding and respecting this order is part of Voodoo, whether in your personal or professional life *(Witches of the Craft)*.

When that sense of order is expanded to the philosophies of life and spirituality, you must also realize that the overwhelming power of the natural world, our space in the ecology of the food chain, the nurturing or harmful effects of flora on our state, and everything surrounding us in the physical world also take part in the hierarchy. Thus, respecting the power of nature, knowledge of the force of a single root to heal or cause damage also becomes a part of Voodoo.

Furthermore, when this sense of order is expanded beyond the physical world into metaphysical and spiritual realms, the spirits that passed on before us, ancestors of our own physical lineages as well as philosophical ancestors to our beliefs, practices, forms of Vodou and other traditional religio-spiritual systems, followed by saints and other notable spirits which possessed "power" in their physical life, as well as non-human beings—whether good or bad, holy or unholy, divine or otherwise—topped finally by deities, all form an up-down system of hierarchy which must be respected and revered.

Thus, in the end, every facet of Voodoo—from spirit possession to divination, and from its rituals, beats, rhythms, and spells to its forms of worship—revolves around understanding the relevance of the wisdom passed down to us without conceit, and appreciating the awesome chasm which lies between someone who is yet to embark on any path of spirituality with someone who has dedicated their life to it. This facet has passed on into the next state of being, and is transmitting that knowledge back down to us mortals with the added benefit of their unmatched experiences of the phases of living and dying.

Moreover, many Vodouisants consider this hierarchy so all-inclusive that they don't differentiate between any forms of their own religion with those of others which may respect and honor elders and the order of the universe. This is why you may also come across many Houngans and Mambos, male and female Vodou priests respectively, who may also be initiated in the ways of Santeria (though they may hate to call it by this name, as this was a Spanish term coined by outsiders) and Candomblé, or many others who may not even differentiate between themselves and followers of other syncretic religions if the question comes to spiritual compatibility or to allow others uninitiated in their ways to take part in rituals or gatherings. Lastly, unlike many other religions where spiritual help is preconditioned upon crossing their exclusive rite of initiation, Voodoo does not ask for seekers of knowledge or spiritual peace to meet pre-set requisites before help, guidance, or even future advice is offered by the spirits to other initiated practitioners in their name. Since everyone is part of the same order, anyone can access its benefits—however, perceiving said benefits yourself requires immense dedication.

Chapter 2: Understanding the Nature of Voodoo Practice

As we discussed before, the basis of Voodoo lies in order. When dealt with in a metaphysical context, it refers to the hierarchy of the entire spiritual world existing above us in the chain or ascendancy. At the top of that chain, Voodoo believes in the existence of a supreme being known as "Bondye" or "Good God"—believed to be derived from the French "Bon Dieu." However, Voodoo practitioners do not ever communicate with the Supreme Deity themselves, since they believe Bondye—also known as Gran Met—to exist in a plane far superior to our own, incommunicable and grander on a scale of thought or perception unimaginable to mortals.

Instead, all communication, worship, reverence, and any other form of spiritual action are aimed at the spiritual world in between primarily ancestors, other "powerful" notables who have passed on, and supremely the "Loa". The Loa act as spirit intermediaries between Bondye and humanity; and unlike the notables and ancestors who are worshipped—they are served. Moreover, Voodoo rejects any notion of heaven or hell, but instead believes in reincarnation of the soul for those who are as yet unable to free themselves from the chains of life. Therefore, the actions performed by someone in this life may lead to lowered states of reincarnation within the next. However, powerful ancestral spirits or other notables with "power"—whether used for good or evil—may either transcend or stay trapped in the spiritual world, becoming part of the Loa, depending on their attributes.

However, the Loa themselves are also innumerable, and so are divided into 21 entire nations—often corresponding to the geographical locations or the united races of tribes from which the belief of said intermediary spirits was derived. Some of the most notable and well-known nations among the 21 are the Rada Loa, Petro Loa, Kongo Loa, Nago Loa, and the Ghede Loa.

Within the ones listed above, the Rada Loa are associated with the older deities of Africa, and are usually considered wiser, more positive, nurturing and more beneficent patriarchs and matriarchs among the spirit world. Among those brought over from the same continent, the Kongo Loa are believed to have originated from the Congo region and include the serpent Loa which make up the Simbi sub sect. Continuing with the same geographical theme, the Nago Loa are said to have originated from the Yoruba in the region of Nigeria and include the various aspects of the Ogun spirits, which are said to be derived from the spirit patron of smelting, hunting, war, and politics.

Moving away from the geographical specificity of Africa, the Petro Loa are usually more warlike than most other Loa "nanchons" or nations, and are more closely associated with the spirits encountered during Vodou's time in Haiti, and during the development of Voodoo in the New World. Last but not least, among the nations of Loa mentioned above, are the Ghede Loa, which are believed to be the spirits of the dead that are led by the famous Barons of Voodoo (the most famous among them being Baron Samedi, derived from the French word for "Saturday"). As spirits which were once mortals, the Ghede Loa are more focused on sense-derived existences than the rest, and consequently display greater sexuality as well as an amplification of human passions—good or bad.

Now before introducing any specific Loa among the Voodoo pantheon for want of a better word, I must start with a prelude. Discard any assumptions you've made about Loa from pop culture misrepresentations. In recent times, one of the most offensively portrayed characters was that of Papa Legba from a popular American horror show. As opposed to the highly insulting portrayal of a drug-snorting, baby-snatching, chaotic spirit representation, Papa Legba is one of the most benevolent and wise spirits in the higher realms, and admirably performs his role as the Gatekeeper beyond the veil of life and death. Papa Legba is the first spirit called upon in any ritual, and is the communicator between our physical realm and that of the spirits. He is the guardian of the Crossroads and

Doorways, and is first politely requested to keep communications open between this world and the *other* in order to fulfill any ritual or spell.

The second thing which I must clear up is the nature of Voodoo practice itself. Unlike "black magic", which is often held to be the popular representation of mainstream Voodoo by writers and directors, Voodoo is the exact antithesis of that. In fact, the dark magic performed in Voodoo is the realm of darker Bokors on the fringes of the Voodoo universe, and they perform what is known as "red magic" instead, because of the belief that people under such spells would have red eyes. Voodoo practitioners take it as their duty to counter such magic and protect others from its evil influences. Almost all Voodoo magic concerns itself either with protection (physical, temporal, metaphysical) or healing (physiological, psychological, spiritual), and that which doesn't fall within those two categories is used to improve the lives of the requisitioners, specifically in ways which wouldn't harm anyone else by doing so.

Now, we've already briefly discussed the role of Papa Legba as the Gatekeeper to the Vilokan—the spiritual realm, which is home to the Loas or Lwa, as well as the dead. However, beyond the role already discussed, Papa Legba is also a nurturer, and the bridge which allows the energy of Bondye to flow into our physical realm.

Moving on to other Lwa, one of the other most important spirits is the Baron—who has many different aspects: La Croix, Samedi, etc. In his singular form, the Baron is the Lord of Death, and the spirit which decides when someone's time is up in the mortal realm. Conversely, he is also the spirit who will refuse to let someone die before their time. As one of his more well-known aspects, Baron Samedi is the ruler of all cemeteries. However, the Baron is used in all manner of Voodoo magic—from good to bad—and his specific aspects vary as largely as the practitioners who wish to call upon him in service to him.

Moving on, for healing Vodouisants, another powerful entity often served is the Gran Bwa, also known as the Loa of the Forest. As the ruler of the green lands, this spirit is widely regarded as an immensely powerful healer, and the holder of all herbal secrets to abundance and good health. However, if what you wish to heal are emotions, then the Loa to call upon and serve is La Sirene of the sea. As an extremely positive spirit, La Sirene cleans away negativities of the emotional kind, and nurtures and strengthens existing bonds.

But, if your needs are more of a physical nature, when you're dealing with problems where you need to overcome or defeat enemies, then one of the aspects of Ogun would be requested to grace you with their presence. As we discussed earlier, Ogun is the lord of smiths, warriors, politicians, etc., and can either endow you with the fortitude to meet your problems head on, the wisdom to solve your problems with your enemies or overcome them if no other viable path shows itself, or can be requested to directly deal with your enemies—if that's the sort of practice in which you wish to involve yourself.

However, these are short and shallow representations of immensely old, powerful, and complex spirits—each of which have eons' worth of folklore behind them. Therefore, instead of looking to provide you with shallow introductions here, I would rather recommend that you spend some time specifically studying up on them—though I will still discuss the necessary spirits to be summoned for the rituals and spells in subsequent chapters. One last piece of advice, which I will offer to any of you sincerely interested in immersing yourself within Voodoo, is to also search for Elders, Mambos, or Houngans within your city or town—not a difficult feat in today's times.

This advice is primarily because, since Voodoo has an inherently esoteric form, there is no single text or literature which manages to capture even an iota of its essence. Also, traditional Vodou, as accepted in its Haitian form, will never recognize your efforts as Voodoo unless you establish some concrete relationship with an elder in the practice—that's simply an unavoidable fact. Moreover, no source or book can teach you into the deeper intricacies of the Lwa like the experiential wisdom of one who has been dealing with them for decades. Since this book is intended as an introduction or a primer, it will be insufficient to fulfill the requirements needed for you to take deeper steps into the practice as well. In fact, we already have our hands pretty full just ensuring that you have sufficient knowledge and wisdom simply performing the most basic spells and rituals correctly, without misfiring or backfiring.

Chapter 3: Preparing Yourself for Spells and Rituals

If you've had any take-away from the discussions in the past two chapters, I hope it's this—Voodoo is a new name for an amalgamation of immensely old systems which can be traced back at least seven thousands years in their making, if not more. However, unlike popular thought that mixing between faith systems somehow muddles up the original message and dilutes them down, Voodoo has only ever incorporated within itself beliefs that resonated with the worldwide wisdom of the ancients—that the Earth and its various component elements are not to be messed with; that there is an order to everything which cannot be ignored or surpassed, regardless of conceit or self deception; that the soul isn't an energy which simply disperses after death, but retains its conscious form long enough to alter the workings of the world.

As an end result, Voodoo has taken the best of each system which encountered it in the past, and has expanded it till every practitioner within its folds can sharpen themselves to a honed spiritual edge depending on their intent, and yet not be able to even scratch the surface of the ultimate wisdom, nature, and understanding of Voodoo as a whole. In fact, any assertion that two practitioners would view Voodoo in the same way if they've had different teachers even in the same geographical neighborhood is entirely erroneous—much less if they were practicing it in different states or nations.

Even when Voodoo was under threat by Christianity in the beginning, it assimilated itself in a way that allowed it to nurture the same age-old bonds with Lwa and their previous beliefs—the only difference being that they equated each Lwa to a corresponding Saint, and took up their traditional prayers for said Lwa on the day attributed to that specific Saint. However, this doesn't mean that they weren't true Christians either, with Popes in the past as well having attended some positive Voodoo rituals, and commenting on the Christian piety of many Vodouisants. That was because the spirituality in this belief system was inherently strong enough to allow themselves to adapt and survive through their rituals, rather than feel insecure about their innate message being lost by adopting the mantle of a threatening religious system. What these seemingly segmented pieces of information is leading up to is this— throw away your notions that this is a spiritual form which can be easily entered, accessed, or even understood by someone unwilling to dedicate immense effort to the cause of unlocking its secrets. However, the spells and rituals may still be powerful enough for some uninitiated foolhardy dummy to cause damage to themselves and the ones they love, through misfired magic. Therefore, there are several preparations required to safely and successfully navigating these complex beginnings, without the hands-on help and guidance of a mentor.

The first thing which you need to understand is that excessive emotions and passions are a hindrance to practice, especially if you're a neophyte. In fact, those who try to break through this block with force of emotions alone may find themselves on the path of Bokors, and away from true Voodoo. That's because you need a calm mind to access the spiritual world, and an absence of ego and pride when conversing with spirits ages older and wiser, and infinitely more powerful than you. Therefore, the very first preparation needs to be engaging in meditative practices to control and overcome emotional turbulences. This will also help you understand and surpass petty fears and insecurities which may lead you down dangerous paths once you gain some proficiency in practice. As well, it will stop you from fighting when you engage in spirit possession after calling upon a Lwa. This is primarily because the main method of communication with spirits is by letting them inside yourself as the medium—though trust me on this, you're still light years away from attempting anything of that sort; said practices only being reliably invoked once you reach the level of priests, which means that you will already have had immense tutoring by Vodouisant mentors. However, it's a good foundation to build upon, and a great framework on which you can construct a positive experience and outlook as a Voodoo practitioner.

The next thing which you need to engage in, before attempting any spell or ritual, is self-purification. This is most commonly achieved through ritual bathing, using ingredients like sage, sandalwood powder, salt, mint, etc. in bath water. The biggest reason for this practice is to rid yourself of all residual negative energies which you may have picked up through touch or association while venturing outside, or even the same from your own surroundings—which is why burning sage at home before attempting any ritual is of primary importance. Other than purification before rituals, another great advantage of ritual bathing is that it can rid you of fatigue or emotional drains which may have latched on to you through outside sources or environments, and will give you a spiritual cleansing that will allow your own positivity to surface in everyday interactions.

The last preparation lies in the making of a Voodoo altar. Now, while you have access to Papa Legba, all the Ghede Lwa, and your ancestral spirits, beyond that the Lwa only respond to those for whom they may have an affinity. Since this differs from person to person, the only accurate way to create an altar dedicated to Lwa who *will* respond to you and will allow you to serve them, is by getting a reading from a mentor or another Voodoo practitioner. The Lwa only respond to people who have character attributes with which the specific spirits themselves can resonate, and so your reading will determine the way your altar looks in the end. Therefore, no, you don't choose the spirits which you serve as a basic practitioner, but rather the spirits choose if they will allow you to serve them.

However, for a *very* basic altar, there are very few requirements—since Papa Legba and the Ghedes are about all that are available to everyone right off the bat. All you need is a clean space—put a white table cloth on it for the Rada side as well as some black and red fabric for the space which specifically denotes Papa Legba, put a cross or crucifix in the center, arrange the symbols of your most beloved ancestors on the other side from the cross. Always have a bowl of clean and pure water, which is to be replaced as often as needed. Keep burning sage and purifying incense whenever you wish to pray to them. Present white flowers to Papa Legba's side, along with funerary flowers to your ancestors. Keep in mind that the flowers have to be real and changed as often as necessary to always keep them fresh. Make sure that the offerings of water and flowers are in separate vessels for each of the sides of your altar. Moreover, if you're creating a side on the altar for Papa Legba—as you always should—draw or recreate his *veve* symbol on a weave and place that at the altar. With this, your basic altar is complete. Aside from them, some of the other required tools are drums to create a conducive energetic atmosphere to incite the chosen spirits into visiting you. However, since you'll probably be a sole practitioner at first, search for specific music and chants dedicated to the spirit of your choice, and play that in the background to create the proper environment.

Chapter 4: Understanding and Using Voodoo Oils

Many Voodoo spells and rituals use oils, especially when it comes to practitioners in the United States. In places such as the Dominican Republic or Haiti, fresh herbs are generally used more often as the more tropical locations tend to have an abundance of plants that have spiritual and/or medicinal properties.

Voodoo spells and rituals might use perfume oils, spiritual oils, or ritual oils. For ritual oils, the strongest oils are those that are hand-made, rather than manufactured in a processing plant. Many spiritual oils are manufactured today, although as with ritual oils they are strongest if they are made by hand using sacred herbs and pure essential oils.

While the different oils are used in different ways, the overall purpose is the same: to connect you to the life force, "Fos" or "Ase", of whichever root, plant, flower, or herb was used to produce the oil. This will allow you to draw on the spiritual or medicinal properties of the plant, and use those properties to enhance or strengthen your spell or ritual.

Spiritual oils and perfume oils are most commonly used by the choosing a specific scent to be worn for a specific spiritual purpose, such as attracting a lover, commanding a situation, or calming and healing. For most purposes, you will be the one wearing the oil; however, there are situations where you will need to surreptitiously transfer the oil to another person. This is usually done with oils that are used to attract a lover or increase passion.

Ritual oils are used to dress Voodoo candles or lights. In order to properly dress a candle, there is a specific process that must be followed. If you are using a jar candle, you must carve the name of the person that you wish to influence into the wax on the top of the candle, and then pour the oil onto the candle (making sure that it seeps into the carved name) and light the candle while casting your spell. This creates the candle as a focal point, which must be worked each day that it burns in order for the spell to succeed. Working the candle means to talk to one's spirit each day, over the candle, about what that particular spell is trying to achieve.

If you are using ritual candles (those created in the form of a figure like a cat or a skull), the process is similar. First, you must carve the name of the person that you are trying to influence, or purpose of the ritual, into the candle. It does not have to be on the top of the candle when working with ritual candles. As an alternative to carving the name or purpose, you can also write your petition on natural paper such as fiber paper or parchment, and place it underneath the candle. Light the candle, pour the ritual oil out onto your hands and rub them together, then rub your hands on the candle. The pouring of the oil onto your hands and rubbing it onto the candle must be done each day to get the most powerful results.

Some Voodoo practitioners, especially those in Haiti, will use oil lamps instead of candles. This allows you to combine several powerful elements, such as oils, powders, wicks made from specific materials, and sacred herbs. The enhanced strength created by the combination of all of these elements will allow you to focus and draw on the Loa to an even greater extent.

There are many places, both online and in-person, where you can purchase these oils if you wish. However, you might also like to make your own. If you do choose to try and make your own oils, you will need to know about carrier oils, because many recipes use carrier oils. A carrier (or base) oil is used to dilute essential oils and 'carry' the herbs or other ingredients that you may be using in a recipe.

There are many different carrier oils that can be used. The most commonly used carrier oils are apricot kernel oil, castor oil, coconut oil, grapeseed oil, hazelnut oil, jojoba oil, olive oil, sunflower seed oil, sweet almond oil, and wheat germ oil. As you will see, most (if not all) of these oils are common household oils that can be easily found in your local grocery store. Some recipes will call for specific carrier oils, while others will work with whichever carrier oil you choose to use.

Now that you know how oils are used and what carrier oils are, we can start to learn about some recipes that you might want to make to produce your own Voodoo oils.

Van Van oil is a commonly used oil, which is used for blessings, purification, and removing negative energies from a place. A common way to use Van Van oil is in floor washes (the Voodoo kind, not the home cleaner kind). To make your own Van Van oil, you will need to gather the following ingredients:

- Sixteen parts lemongrass oil
- Eight parts citronella oil
- One part palmarosa oil
- One part vetivert oil
- Pyrite (Fool's Gold)
- Dried lemongrass

The lemongrass oil and citronella oil are essential for making Van Van oil; the Palmarosa and vetivert oils will make the Van Van oil more powerful if you use them, but they are not essential.

Blend the four oils together, mixing them well, and then let the concoction sit in a dark location for at least one week. After the week has passed, stir in a pinch or two of dried lemongrass, and add a few tiny crystals of the Fool's Gold. Then pour the mixture into a bottle, and you have your Van Van oil.

Another kind of oil that is commonly used in Voodoo spells is Black Cat oil. This oil is frequently used to break hexes and make gambling charms, and it can also be used in love spells. In order to make your own Black Cat oil, you will need the following ingredients:

- Two parts bay, or bay laurel, oil
- Two parts clary sage oil
- One part myrrh oil
- Tiny pieces of steel wool, or some other type of iron shavings
- Tiny pieces of solid myrrh resin
- Fur from a black cat

Once you have gathered the ingredients together, simply mix them all up and pour the concoction into a bottle. Then you will have made your own Black Cat oil.

One type of oil that is very useful for practitioners is Blessing oil, which is used to bless and purify your altar and tools. To make this oil, blend the following ingredients:

- ½ oz. frankincense powder
- ½ oz. benzoin powder

Take two tablespoons of the mixture and add it to 2 oz. of whichever carrier oil you would like. Bottle the combination, and your Blessing oil is ready to be used.

If you are casting a spell in which you are trying to banish a spirit, this Banishing oil recipe will come in handy:

- ½ oz. olive oil
- Twelve drops rue essential oil
- Fifteen drops pine essential oil
- Seven drops pepper oil
- Ten drops peppermint oil
- Crushed black pepper corns
- Chip of black onyx or obsidian

This recipe is most effective when mixed during a waning moon.

Divination oil is used to open up your psychic vision and improve your clarity of vision. Place the oil on your forehead (your third eye) and your temples for best effect. To make Divination oil, mix the following ingredients:

- One part ambergris oil
- One part musk oil
- Two parts violet (crushed dried petals)
- Two parts vetivert
- Four parts lilac (crushed dried blooms)

Add the ingredients to two oz. of hazelnut oil or coconut oil.

If you are looking to protect and defend yourself against magical or spiritual attacks, Protection oil is what you need. Take the Protection oil and dab it on your doors and windows to guard against the danger. The following oils will be required to prepare your Protection oil:

- Five drops of black pepper OR four drops of basil
- Five drops of petitgrain
- Three drops of geranium
- Two drops of pine
- One drop of vetivert

There is a type of oil for every type of Voodoo ritual that you might wish to carry out. Seek a local practitioner or look online – the resources are out there if you look for them. While purchasing the oils is a perfectly acceptable way to obtain them, making your own will allow you to ensure the quality of the oil and will allow you to be more closely connected to the ritual that you are performing.

Chapter 5: Understanding and Using Voodoo Candles and Powders

In the chapter above, we discussed the use of Voodoo oils, which is often combined with the use of candles. In this chapter, you will learn more about the use of candles in Voodoo, as this is an important element of the practice of Voodoo.

Candles have been a part of Voodoo magic as long as Voodoo has been practiced. In fact, flame plays a role in most of the world's religions, which makes sense as fire has always been one of the most important tools for survival for humankind. In Voodoo, candles are used in ceremonies and rituals, and also in spell casting. They can also be used as charms themselves – to do so, simply inscribe the relevant symbol on the candle, then let it burn.

There are two main aspects of candles that assist with rituals and spells: the flame, and the color of the candle. The flame helps to put you into a meditative frame of mind, which assists with concentrating on your intention. Each color of a candle has a different association, so it is important to choose the candle color that is most appropriate for the type of ritual or spell that you are carrying out.

The following is a list of the different colors in which Voodoo candles come, along with an explanation of the purpose or association of each color. It is important to note that any color can be used for positive or negative rituals or spells – it is up to you as the user to decide which you will do.

- Red – passion, affection, love, physical vitality
- White – purity, spiritual blessings, rest, healing
- Green – gambling luck, money, work, business, crops
- Purple – power, control, ambition
- Black – dark thoughts, repelling, sorrow
- Yellow – prayer, money, devotion, attraction, happiness
- Orange – opening a pathway, changing plans, prophecy
- Dark blue – depression, moodiness, negative situations
- Light blue – harmony, peace, joy, kindness
- Pink – romance, attraction, healthy lifestyle
- Brown – neutrality, court proceedings
- Red and Black combined – returning evil to its sender

As discussed in the chapter above, once you have chosen a properly colored candle you will need to anoint it with an oil that is appropriate for your purpose. If you are casting a positive spell (such as attraction) you should rub the oil onto the candle from the wick to the base, moving your hands toward you. If you are casting a negative spell, such as a curse or to repel someone, rub the oil onto the candle from the base to the wick, moving your hands away from you. When using a Voodoo candle in a ritual or spell, make sure to allow the candle to burn down completely unless the recipe calls for something different.

There are many different Voodoo rituals and spells that involve candles. One of the most popular resources, which sets out many of these rituals, is Henry Gamache's Master Book of Candle Burning, first published in 1942. However you can also find many rituals online, and if you work with a practiced Vodoun they will be able to teach you many rituals as well.

Some rituals involve only one candle, and one or two types of oils, and are quite straight-forward. Others require several candles and oils, and may even involve moving the candles around to different positions throughout the ritual. It is usually best to start with more simple rituals, so that you can become accustomed to the use of candles and ensure that you are carrying out the rituals properly, before attempting the more complex rituals or spells.

Once you have carried out a Voodoo candle ritual or spell, you can further increase the power and effectiveness of the ritual or spell by sprinkling a powder on the candle. Voodoo powders are usually made from a base of talc that is then blended with different powdered mineral and herbal ingredients depending on the intention of the powder.

Generally speaking, powders will contain the same basic ingredients (or at least ingredients from the same sources) as the oils of the same name or purpose. So for example, Fast Luck oil contains vanilla, cinnamon, and wintergreen, and those same components are used to prepare the Fast Luck powder.

There are also basic powders which are made of only one ingredient, and can be used to amplify any ritual or spell that has the same general purpose. Ground egg shell powder can be used for purification, salt works well for protection, sugar assists with sweetening one's disposition, and red brick dust will amplify warding rituals or spells. Graveyard dirt is a quite common type of powder, and the appropriate use will vary depending on from whose grave the dirt came.

The genesis of the use of powders in Voodoo magic is a long-held belief in many African cultures that the act of placing one's foot on an object could lead to contamination of oneself by the energy of that object. Initially looked at as a negative consequence, the possibility eventually was developed that it could be used to intentionally absorb the energy of various components and refocus that energy on one's intended goal.

While powders are often added to candle or oil rituals or spells, they can be used on their own for some purposes. The advantage of powders over candles or oils is that powders are not generally easily detected, so they can be used without alerting others to what you are doing. So if you are applying for a job, for example, you may choose to dust or trace some luck powder onto the application; the powder is unlikely to be detected (especially if you clean off the residue), whereas an oil splotch on a piece of paper would be fairly noticeable.

One popular way of using powders is to blow the powder in the four directions. This must be done in a specific order: North, South, West, and then East. This practice places you at the center of the magic's crossroads, so to speak, so that all possibilities and pathways are open to you and your magic can travel as you wish.

Another common use of powders to is place a powder in each of the four corners of a room, which will protect the space within from negative energy. If you are using a powder to curse someone, you could place the powder at the outside four corners of that individual's home.

Just like with Voodoo oils, you can purchase Voodoo powders online or in-person, or you could make your own. In order to prepare a powder, simply grind the ingredients with mortar and pestle – or for the more modern Vodoun, a coffee grinder – then add a bit of carrier oil or essential oil (depending on the recipe) and mix the combination with a base of corn starch or rice flour.

You can also use paint powder if you would like to amplify your powder with the energy from the color that you choose. Talc can be used instead of corn starch or rice flour, and is the base most commonly used in commercial products, but corn starch and rice flour are more easily found in your local grocery store and are safer around children or people who might be sensitive to inhalants.

As you can no doubt imagine, there is a powder for every purpose, just as there is an oil for every purpose. The following are some powders that you might be interested in using.

Dream Powder

Dream powder can be sprinkled on your bedding before you go to bed, to assist you with having prophetic dreams. The ingredients for this powder are licorice, cardamom, cinnamon, and coriander. Use the same approximate amount of each. If you need to break a hex or send evil back to its sender, prepare a powder from rose, vetivert, frankincense, and honeysuckle.

Gambling Luck Powder

If you wish to be lucky at gambling, combine the following ingredients:

- One tsp of carnation petals (dried and powdered)
- One oz. of powdered sandalwood
- One tsp of powdered cinnamon
- ½ dram of myrrh oil
- ½ dram of frankincense oil

Combine the ingredients with four oz. of cornstarch, and grind together.

Money Making Powder

If you are seeking to improve your chances at making money, then you can make a money drawing powder. To make this powder, combine and grind the following ingredients:

- ¼ tsp powdered cinnamon
- One oz. powdered sandalwood
- One tsp yellow dock
- One tbsp. powdered five-finger grass
- ¼ dram of patchouli oil
- ½ dram of frankincense oil
- ¼ dram of myrrh oil

Combine the ingredients with four oz. of cornstarch or rice flour, and grind together.

Hot Foot Powder

This powder is used to get rid of someone in your life – not in any way that will injure them, but it will likely be permanent. While it does not cause any harm, it is a powerful spell and the ritual should be practiced very carefully. If the spell backfires it could end up making you go away – i.e. you could lose your job, your relationship, etc. So use this recipe at your own risk, and make sure that the person causes you enough grief that it is worth the risk to use this spell.

Candles and powders play an important role in the practice of Voodoo, and you should make sure to familiarize yourself with the different options so that you ensure that you are using the best and most effective elements for every spell, ritual, or ceremony that you perform.

First, gather the following ingredients, in relatively equal proportions, and grind them together to form the powder:

- Cayenne or habanero pepper
- Black pepper
- Sulfur
- Salt

Once you have the powder, you will also need a bowl for holding the powder, a small jar, four black candles, two black rush lights, and a drum or some kind of rhythm instrument. Rush lights are a type of candle made by dipping rushes into tallow or wax. They are quite long and can be very fragile, so handle them carefully.

Purify and bless your altar, and set up the items listed above. Arrange the black candles so that your altar is well lit; do not use any other color of candles during this spell. For added effect, you can drape the altar in black and/or wear black yourself.

Pour a small spoonful of the Hot Foot Powder into the bowl, and set the bowl onto the altar. Place the black rush lights at either side of the bowl, and light them while focusing intently on the source of your problem. Using the rhythm instrument (or your hands, if you wish to clap them) start up a fairly urgent beat. To that beat, chant: "You shall rise, you shall rise. You shall walk and you shall fly. Out of my life and away – onward, outward, away be gone. Trouble me no more, I give you no power. You have no power, no power over me." (*Witches of the Craft*)

Repeat this chant over and over, focusing on the problem individual and putting your passion into it. Continue to chant until the rush lights have burned down, then take the bowl in both of your hands and focus on sending all of your energy into it. Visualize the power boiling and bubbling with your emotion and energy. Once you feel that you have directed your energy into the powder, pour the powder into the jar and close the jar tightly.

To complete the spell, you must scatter the powder in the path of your target, without being seen. Pour the powder into your hand, then use blow on the powder to spread it over an area where the person walks on a regular basis. This spell is very focused on that one individual, so you do not need to worry about it affecting anyone else who may walk in that area.

Each of these oils and powders has a specific way in which it can be applied to enhance or improve your spells. Make sure to know the different oils and powders and how they can be used, so that you achieve the best effects possible when you are conducting your Voodoo rituals.

Chapter 6: Learning the Basic Voodoo Spells

One thing that you'll soon learn is that while preparations for spells may be complicated, the usual spells themselves will be quite easy to perform.

For this spell, what you will need to learn about first is the creation of your own Voodoo doll. Now, again through the mishandlings of pop culture, people assume Voodoo dolls to be tools for evil made to harm target(s). However, that couldn't be farther from the truth. In fact, many good practitioners use Voodoo dolls as a way of attaching positive herbs and cleansing agents to those who have requested aid, in order to purge them of negative forces and protect them from evil when required. Again, the materials are attached to the dolls with pins. However, said pins don't hurt or harm the targets of the doll, but are instead used to join the effects of the attached objects and talismans to the essence of the represented person. A normal ritual, even using pins, on a Voodoo doll made to represent someone else *cannot* harm them in any way.

Dolls can either be used to denote a specific person, or may be representative of a type of problem you yourself wish to banish. Therefore, if you're planning on conducting emotionally healing rituals, or even just a protection spell, you can create a Voodoo doll for that specific purpose.

The first thing which you need to do is to gather the ingredients of the doll itself—most of which *have* to be made from natural material collected from nature, such as organic fabrics, wood, bark, grass, twigs, etc. However, that doesn't mean that you can't use beads, buttons, glue, etc., in its construction either— especially if you're making it to resemble someone. Once you've gathered the material, wrap it all in organic fabric, dig a hole in your backyard, and bury it for a few days to allow the earth to sap away all negative energies within the materials, whether organic or synthetic. Once you've done that, take it out, burn some sage, and make sure to lightly expose it to all the ingredients within the smoke of the sage plant to cleanse it thoroughly. Only handle these steps after you've completed your ritual bathing.

Once the cleansing is over, it's time to make the doll. Within its creation, the phases of the moon sometimes makes a difference in the efficacy of the doll's operations—the waxing moon being great for dolls which will be used to conjure benefits or protection, and the waning moon being better suited for dolls dealing with expulsion of negative energies and forces. Select some up-tempo instrumental music in the background, preferably with traditional drums, to allow yourself to meditate on the task at hand and enter a focused state. The importance of focus is that, while making the doll, the purpose of its creation should be foremost in your mind and it should stay that way till you're done making it. Use your imagination to visualize the outcome you seek with the doll, and you'll imbue it with your power to make that image come true—thus turning it into an effective Voodoo tool.

After having created it, you need to cleanse it once more by passing it through the smoke of positive or protective herbs. After this is done, your Voodoo doll is complete, but should be cleansed once more before use if you intend to store it away. Moreover, if you've made the doll to represent a specific person, anoint it in their name with water in order to grant the doll its "identity", and don't store it for too long. While doing so, invoke the name as identity of the doll with the image of the person at the forefront of your mind, and speak clearly as to the purpose for which the spiritual connection between the doll and the human has been invoked. Moreover, whichever way you intend to use it, clearly and decisively welcome the doll as a treasured object which will bring you luck and success in your endeavors, and will serve to protect/bring luck/bring love/heal its original, or whatever other specific reason may exist behind its conjuration. Do not create dolls which represent others, unless you plan to use it for sure.

Once you have created your Voodoo doll, there are many ways in which you can use it. A doll can work as a focusing tool in meditation and ritual, simply by holding the doll in your hand while you concentrate on your intention or goal. Alternatively, you can put the doll onto your altar and keep your gaze on it while concentrating.

Another way in which to use a Voodoo doll is in candle rituals or spells. To use a Voodoo doll in this way, choose a candle that is appropriate for your purpose and carry out the candle ritual as usual, using the candle technique where you write your intention or goal on a piece of paper. Then hold your doll in your hands and focus with intensity on your goal or purpose. Once you feel that you have concentrated sufficiently, place the doll next to the candle and allow the candle to burn down completely. Once the candle has burned down, remove the petition and attach it to your doll. After nine days have passed, burn the petition and then scatter the ashes to the East.

You can also use a Voodoo doll with the seven pins, which is the method most commonly shown in pop culture. Alternatives for pins include needles, nails, or fish bones. The seven pins are each a different color, and each color represents a different aspect. Yellow is success, white is positivity, red is power, purple is spirituality, green is money, blue is love, and black is for repelling negative energy.

To carry out the seven pins ritual, select the color of pin that best represents your intention or goal. Place a pin in the applicable portion of the doll: head for issues dealing with knowledge, heart for emotional concerns, and stomach for intuitive purposes. For example, if you wanted to improve the power of the person at whom you are aiming the ritual, then you would select a red pin and place it into the head of your doll.

You can also use your Voodoo doll to petition a particular Loa to assist you with your request. To do this, choose a candle in a color that is appropriate to the Loa whom you are petitioning, and make an offering of the Loa's favorite things in the Loa's favorite number. Performing the ritual at your altar after properly preparing it – including purification and blessing – will give you the best results.

For example, if you wanted to petition Papa Legba, you would choose black or red candle (but not black and red), and greet him with the ritual greeting where you state his name, ask him to open the door, and state that on the way back, you will return the favor. Then communicate what you would like and offer him three of one of his favorite things – candy, rum, or cigars.

You should be aware that when you use a doll to petition a Loa, you are essentially placing an order with that Loa, which then creates a contract between you and the Loa. Your part of that contract is to do whatever is under your control, in your life, to help to achieve the goal; the Loa's part is to do whatever he, she, or it has control over in order to assist you.

Basic Healing Charm

For this basic spell, the stuffing of the doll needs to be plain white fabric. Along with it you'll also need an amber colored semi-precious stone, which is often used for healing. As well, collect and keep eucalyptus, rosemary, and basil to burn at the altar. Take a few strands of your own hair, wrap them around the stone, and sew them both into the head of the doll. Also sew some of the healing herbs in the space of your doll correspondent to the area which needs healing, possibly around the heart and lungs if you have a regular infection. Once the preparation is done, simply light the herbs and leave them and the charm doll at the altar till you feel better. However, once you're done, and feel healthier, purify the doll with burning sage smoke, thank it for its help, and preferably let it flow away in a body of clean running water if there is one around. If not, bury it in soft earth, but far away from your own property after having removed your hair and the stones from the inside.

Money Spell

For this spell, you will require the following items:

- Your Voodoo doll
- A piece of green flannel cloth
- Three of each of the coin denominations of your country – in the United States, for example, you would need three pennies, three dimes, and three-quarters
- Three cloves
- three cinnamon sticks
- One whole nutmeg
- three whole allspice
- A gold bell
- A straight pin that has a green head
- Three pieces of candy

Take all of the items other than your doll, bell, and pin, and wrap them in the green flannel cloth, then attach the cloth to your doll. This has the effect of 'sealing' the items. Use the straight pin to attach the gold bell to your Voodoo doll. Shake the doll with your non-dominant hand for nine minutes, while reciting an incantation to Papa Legba.

The exact words of the incantation do not matter – you need to ensure that you ask him to open the door and clear a path for you, to bring you money and the opportunity to make money, and to remove obstacles to wealth. You must also state that in return for his assistance, you will pay him with the candy, then thank him for his help.

Banishing Your Enemies

If you have someone who has been threatening or bothering you, you can use your Voodoo doll to carry out a ritual to banish that person. This involves petitioning one of the Loa for assistance – usually Ogun or Chango, or Erzulie Dantor for women who are victims of domestic violence. The items used in the ritual will depend on which Loa you are petitioning because they each have different favorite items which should be offered.

Chango is the deity of thunder, fire, wars, power, and lightning, and he also represents sensual pleasure. He can assist you with defeating your enemies, gaining power over others, and generally being victorious in your pursuits.

To create an altar for Chango, it is best to use your business desk or a fireplace mantel – power or fire are elements that Chango relates to. Use one or more of each of the following:

- Patron saint – St. Jerome or St. Barbara
- Items associated with places – sky, trees, Trinidad
- Colors for cloth and/or beads – white and red
- Animals and objects – rams, horses, pheasants, turtles, wood, machete, double axe
- Food – yams, apples, peppers, corn
- Planet – Sun or Mars
- Ritual greeting – Kabiosile or Kaguo

Chango's favorite number and day are 6 and Friday, respectively, so it is best to use 6 of items from each category and to carry out the ritual on a Friday when possible.

Once you have gathered all of the items and prepared the altar, light a white candle, then hold the doll in your hand as a focusing tool, as discussed above. Concentrate on what you wish to achieve, and ask Chango to help you with your goal. Make an offering of his favorite items to Chango, at the altar, for the three days following your initial ritual.

Chakra Spell

This spell can be used to direct positive or negative energy at someone, depending on what you wish to do. We will discuss the positive approach in this book – using the pins in a slightly different manner than discussed above, to positively influence the Chakras of someone.

To carry out this spell, prepare a Voodoo doll as above, making sure to anoint it so that it is connected to the person whom you are hoping to affect. Once you have the doll, get into a comfortable position – usually one where you are sitting at or near your altar.

State your intention, and why you are doing it, out loud using your clearest voice. You can state the intention in your regular, everyday language, or use a spell or rhyme format – the choice is yours, use whichever makes you feel most comfortable.

Once you have stated your intention, take the white pin and place it into the top of the doll's head. At the same time, explain what the pin is supposed to do – increase spiritual enlightenment and enable the person to expel negative energies. Proceed through the ritual by placing the rest of the pins into the doll in the following order, each time explaining what the pin is intended to do:

- Purple – forehead, to assist with psychic awareness
- Blue – throat – make the person's goals a reality
- Green – heart – increase a person's health or emotional power

- Yellow – solar plexus increase the person's knowledge and ability to understand
- Orange – stomach – allows the person to deal with whatever comes their way
- Red – base of spine – increases the person's ability to survive the obstacles that they face.

You can use variations on each of the above themes, as long as they generally relate to the overall purpose of each location.

Once you have placed all of the pins, put the doll onto your altar. Starting the next day, remove the red pin; each following day remove one more pin, in the reverse order that they were placed. After you have removed the last pin, the spell is finished.

If there is one specific goal or intention, or only a few, that you wish to focus on, you can carry out the spell by just placing the relevant pins, although always in the same order as stated above – simply skip any colors that you will not be using.

Passion Spell

Not exactly a love spell (those will be dealt with later in the book), the Passion spell is meant to be used to increase the already-existing passion between you and your lover.

To conduct the Passion spell, you will need the following ingredients:

- Three drops of lavender oil
- Three drops of hot pepper sauce
- Orris root pieces
- Whole peppercorns
- Rosemary
- Three cups of rain water

For this spell, the exact amount of the herbs (Orris root, peppercorns, and rosemary) is not important as long as they are in relatively equal proportions to each other.

Pour all of the ingredients into a bowl and stir. While stirring, concentrate on the heat of the hot pepper sauce, and the passion that you are seeking to magnify.

Once the concoction is well-stirred, sprinkle it around your front doorstep or entrance using your fingers. Make sure to cover the entrance well – steps and walkway should also be covered. You should be aware that this spell will probably be less effective if you live in an apartment, because the front entrance to your home is shared with others.

Happiness Spell

This ritual involves petitioning Papa Legba to open the gateway to the spirit world, so that you can ask Oshun for her assistance. Oshun is an African goddess or spirit of love, dance, and art. She has the ability to help provide your emotional strength with a solid foundation so that it is able to grow and prosper.

Start at your altar, with candles in Oshun's favorite colors (green, yellow, or pink) and cinnamon (Oshun's favorite smell) incense burning. First you must ask Papa Legba to help you to open the gateway to the spirit world; in order to do this, make a recitation to Papa Legba to open the door and remind him that his children are waiting. Say the recitation three times in total – Papa Legba's favorite number is three.

Once you have completed the recitation to Papa Legba, hold your Voodoo doll in your hands to be used as a focusing tool. Focus intensely on your desired goal, and say the appropriate ritual greeting for Oshun: Ori Ye Ye O. Then state out loud your desired goal; this can be accompanied by a written petition as well, but it must be stated out loud in order to be effective.

After the initial ritual, continue to make offerings to Oshun for the next three days. Oshun's favorite items include honey, cinnamon, pumpkins, oranges, mirrors, gold, and French pastries. Her favorite number is five, so it will help to make offerings in the amount of five of any item being offered. Finally, her favorite day is Thursday, so this ritual will be most effective if it is begun on a Thursday.

When the ritual has been completed and the additional three days have passed, take the doll and place it in your bedroom or your kitchen, as these are Oshun's favorite rooms of the house.

Stand Tall Spell

This spell will give you a little push during the day when you are feeling insecure or unsure of yourself. All you need are a few ingredients that are easy to find:

- Three sticks, six to eight inches long
- Rough string or heavy twine
- Sturdy nail
- One dried chili pepper

This spell is most effective if you use branches or twigs, but you can also use Popsicle sticks or dowels if that is what you can find.

Using the twine, tie the three sticks together so that they roughly form the shape of the letter 'A'. The cross-piece should be attached near the top so that the shape also resembles a person.

Tie the nail to one leg and the chili pepper to the other – it does not matter which. Wrap the doll's head and limbs with the twine. Then place the doll somewhere in your home that is important to you, and where you will see it on a daily basis. Make sure that the doll is placed so that it is standing upright.

These spells are just some of the spells available to you if you learn how to properly use a Voodoo doll. It is extremely important that you are careful to prepare your doll properly, so that you will achieve the effects that you are seeking. An improperly made doll will not only not allow the spell to work, it could potentially backfire and cause effects that you were not looking for and do not wish to see. But if you do make your doll properly, your spell will be powerful and effective, and you will see the results that you desire.

Chapter 7: Advanced Spells for Protection

The most effective way of creating a basic protection charm to ward off negative energies is to create a protection charm bag. The only things you need to make this are a red drawstring bag, some Angelica herb, aquamarine and sardonyx semi-precious stones, pieces of your hair and nail, and a written prayer simply requesting the spirits to protect you from general physical or mental harm, and bad luck.

Once you've collected the items, first purify each of them by lightly washing them in salted water. After drying, smoke them with burning sage to purify the energies. Of course, this doesn't count for the herbs and the written prayer, which will only need the burning smoke to sufficiently cleanse them for the charm.

After having done that, sit in front of your altar with all the materials in front of you. Make sure that they're placed on the altar right after drying and cleansing to avoid any negative residual energies from around the house or room.

With that, sit and call upon Papa Legba to allow you to communicate with the spirit world. The chant to call upon Papa Legba is as follows:

Papa Legba, Open the gates for me; Atibon Legba, Open the gates for me; Papa open the gates for me to pass; When I come back I will thank the Lwa!

Keep repeating this till you feel a change in the atmosphere. The change could be as drastic as a strong feeling or emotion, or even as small as a tiny shiver running along your spine or goosebumps appearing on your skin. Whatever the change may *feel* like, it is indubitably a good sign, so mentally interpret it as such. If you're very lucky, you may also feel as if you're suddenly in the company and guidance of a warm and caring patriarch.

Once the change is realized, and the spirit world is open, read out your written prayer. Chant it over and over again as you place each item carefully in the bag. In the case of your hair, you can place them in together, put everything else in *one* by *one*, even your nails! After it's over, ask the spirits to bless the bag, thank the spirits for their attention and blessings, and slowly close the bag. Then, keep repeating, "*Papa Legba, I have returned; I thank the Lwa; Papa Legba I have returned, please close the gates; Papa Legba, I have returned, I thank the Lwa*".

And keep repeating it till you feel another shift, and the space around *feels* normal again.

Once this is done, do *not* open the bag again. However, after about a week, wash the bag in salt water, and discard it in a place under the earth and far away from the personal property of others'. This is to avoid decomposition from tainting your bag with negative energies. If you can get pure sea or rock salt, you can swap out the Angelica herb in the bag with it. However, in exchange for not needing to make a new bag each week, the trade off will be that it will be less powerful.

This is a basic protection charm that can be quite useful in providing general protection. There are other Voodoo spells that will help you to protect yourself from more specific threats, or in specific situations. There are spells that protect you by making you spiritually invisible, or by attracting good spirits who will help to shield you or fight on your behalf. You can also choose to reflect the evil or negative energy back toward the person who sent it to you, or by killing the negative energy where it lies.

Protection Pour

This spell can help to protect you from unwanted magic entering your home. This spell must be performed on the night of the dark moon, also known as the new moon. You will need the following ingredients:

- One cup of pure water
- Black ink
- Four or five black whole peppercorns
- Splash of vodka
- Pinch of graveyard dirt
- Red candle

The first step is to light the red candle. Then mix all of the other ingredients together in a bowl that is made from metal, glass, or ceramic. Stir the ingredients only with your left hand's index finger. While you are stirring, call out to Papa Legba to protect your home.

Go to your front door and pour the concoction over the steps and walkway coming up to the front door. Make sure that the area is well covered. The spell can be refreshed by pouring vodka over the area each night of the new moon.

Ban Negative Magical Energies Spell

This spell can be used to prevent negative magic energies from entering your home or a place that you designate. All that you will need is salt and a ritual knife. You will also need to know how to call for Papa Legba, asking him to open the gateway to the spirit world to you and reminding him that his children are waiting. This chant should be repeated continuously while you are conducting the ritual.

Starting at the entrance to your home, or the designated place, sprinkle a thin line of salt at each opening then bash the knife against the opening's left side, halfway up the opening. Using a horizontal motion, move the knife to the right side of the entrance and bash the knife three times against the right side. Continue to each opening or entrance of the location, moving clockwise, until you have reached the first entrance again. At that entrance, draw a second thin line of salt. Through the salt, scratch an X and then an upright cross.

If you are casting the spell at an open location that does not have walls, you will need to sprinkle a thin line of salt in a circle around the entire area, moving clockwise. As you sprinkle the salt hold the knife at chest height. The 'entrance' or starting point is arbitrary.

Once you have completed the circles around the entrances, then move to the center of the home or location and continue your chants to Papa Legba. Ask him to protect the location from negative energies or influences, while visualizing a blinding light spreading from the floor in the center up and out to the walls and entrances.

This spell will protect you from energy attacks by others, unless the caster has a personal object of yours (or of the person who resides in the location). The spell will also not be effective if the person casting the spell against you is already inside the location – nothing can come in, but nothing can get out, so the spell stays inside with you.

Business Protection

This spell will help you to protect your business, such as preventing competitors from stealing your customers or your ideas. The charm that you make during this ritual can be carried on your person or set by your computer or workspace. You will need nine pecans and a small green box or pouch. Pecans are often used in spells involving money or business interests because they symbolize wealth. Nine pecans are used in this ritual because nine is the number of completions and achievements.

To conduct this ritual, shell each pecan and then slowly eat them while visualizing the outcome that you desire. Whether you want to gain more customers, prevent customers leaving you for a competitor, come up with a great new business idea, etc., you must choose your goal and visualize it clearly. Once you have eaten all of the pecans, gather them and place them in the box or pouch. Put the box or pouch somewhere near your work area where it will not be found.

If you use this spell before you open to the public, it will help you to enjoy all of the prosperity and success that you deserve. If you are using it after you have already opened your business, it will help to amplify the success of your business. You can use this spell anytime after you have started your business, even if you have been operating for years.

Pet Protection Spell

As any pet owner knows, protecting your pet is vitally important. You want to make sure that they are safe and healthy at all times, just like you would with any member of your family. For this spell, you will need a purple candle and jasmine incense – the color purple appeals to the entities that love and protect animals, while the scent of jasmine will attract the ancient Egyptian goddesses who worshiped cats. The spell should be conducted on a Friday.

Make sure that your pet is in the room with you when you conduct the spell. Light the candle, using a lighter and not a match – the sulfur from the match flame can add negative energy to the spell. Then light the incense.

Visualize your pet surrounded by a purple light, protected wherever it might go. Allow the candle to burn down completely, while visualizing your protected pet. Once the candle has burned down, bury the stub under the biggest tree in your yard, under the largest root that is closest to your home.

Each of these protection spells can be used in different circumstances. It will be up to you to learn and understand the spells well enough to know which spell to use in your particular circumstances. Choosing a spell that is not appropriate to the situation will not improve the situation, and may even make it worse. So choose carefully and make sure to carry out your chosen spell properly so that you achieve the best effects possible

Chapter 8: Advanced Spells for Revenge

Safe Revenge Spell

This spell is a great way to serve some karma on someone who has hurt you, while remaining safe yourself and staying in a good karmic state. Because you are simply serving them with whichever karma you deserve, it will only affect your karma in a positive way. There are many revenge spells out there, and some can involve serious negative energy – I highly recommend using this spell, because it intended to benefit those around the individual at whom it is directed, and will even benefit the individual in the long run if they allow it do so.

Think of the person who you are trying to affect. Focus on their shortcomings, and also their 'higher self' or the person whom they could be if they chose to follow a positive path rather than a negative one. Next, select a positive quality that would create damage and conflict in their lives (because of their negative traits) but would improve the overall situation.

An excellent example of this is bestowing a conscience on someone who is a vicious criminal – it would be great for the people around the criminal if he or she developed a conscience, but it would obviously make their criminal activities hard for them to carry out.

Remember when conducting this spell that if it is done properly, that positive quality could come back at your up to threefold, so make sure to choose a positive quality that you need or that would not cause conflict in your own life.

Once you have focused on the person, their shortcomings, and the positive quality that you want to send their way, then light one simple candle at your altar and sit down in front of it. State the person and describe their higher self, then the positive trait that you are hoping to bestow.

Use the following incantation: "Upon the planes in which I live, the gift of [*quality you are bestowing*] I now give to [*name of person the spell is directed at*] with all my heart and soul, to change him/her and make him/her whole. By all on high and law of three, this is my will so shall it be." (*Magic Spells and Potions.*)

Focus on the candle and visualize the person with as much concentration as you can manage, then blow out the candle.

Payback Spell

As stated above, and as indicated by its name, the Safe Revenge spell is the safest spell that you can use to wreak some kind of revenge. There are many other revenge spells, though, and depending on the circumstances you may wish to choose one that operates differently than the Safe Revenge spell. The Payback spell is an excellent example of these other options.

For this spell, you will need:

- Black fabric
- Red string or thread
- A drawing or photograph of the person whom you are targeting (if using a drawing, it must be very specific and clearly identify some distinguishing features, and must have the person's name written on it)
- Minimum one handful of graveyard dirt
- Dried patchouli

Start by making the Voodoo doll: cut two person-like shapes from the black fabric, and sew them together with the red thread or string. Also use the red string to sew two X's where the eyes would go. Sew the two pieces together very well, leaving just a small hole for now into which you can put the stuffing.

Take the drawing or picture and rip it up into little pieces. Stuff the pieces into the doll, along with the graveyard dirt and patchouli. Shake the doll so that the contents are mixed well, then sew the doll up completely. Bend the two arms together in front of the doll and sew the doll's hands together. Then bury the doll so that is facing upside down, in a location behind your home.

Mojo Mirror

This spell uses a mirror's reflective power to return negative energy to a person who deserves it, or who initially directed that energy at you. The intention of this spell is that its results will closely reflect what that person did to you first.

You will need the following items:

- Small mirror with no frame
- Black paint
- Paintbrush
- Cloth or dish
- Dark rum

This spell must be performed after nightfall, although you do not have to be in the dark to perform it – you can do it inside with the lights on, if you would like to be at your altar. Pour the rum out over the mirror, and leave the mirror lying on a cloth or in a dish until the rum has dried. Once the rum is dry, paint a thick 'X' on the mirror's face using the black paint.

Say the name of your target five times then smash the mirror. You may want to smash it over a cloth or newspaper so that the broken glass can be easily cleaned up. Gather up all of the mirror fragments and throw them into the garbage.

Hex Removal

If you already have a hex or curse that has been placed against you, you can remove it and protect yourself from it in the future using this spell. You will need the following items:

- At least one large handful of dirt
- Five black peppercorns
- At least five feathers
- Five mustard seeds (whole)
- Five pieces of myrrh resin
- One black candle

Using a medium-sized bowl, place the feathers, mustard, pepper, and myrrh into the bottom of the bowl. Fill the rest of the bowl with the dirt, packing it tightly. Place the candle in the center of the bowl and push it down into the dirt so that it stands upright. Light the candle, and holding your hands over your head order the hex or negative energy to leave you and return to the person who sent it.

Each of these revenge spells can be effective if you are seeking revenge against someone. However, as I said at the beginning of this chapter, if you are seeking revenge on someone I would encourage you to use the safe revenge spell if you must seek revenge. That spell is the only one of these revenge spells that will not negatively impact your own karma, and it will still have the type of effect that you would like to see on your target while also benefiting those around the person.

Chapter 9: Advanced Spells for Love

Love spells are controversial within the practice of Voodoo, just as they are in the various other religions that practice similar magic. Love spells are also one of the most common types of rituals practiced in Voodoo. Some practitioners will think nothing of casting a love spell for themselves or someone else, regardless of the potential consequences. However, it is extremely important that you understand what exactly is involved in love spells, and what the potential consequences are.

One potential danger is that your soul can become bound to the person at whom you have directed the spell. If you are casting a spell for lust, or to have someone love you whom you do not wish to love, then you are taking the chance that you will be bound to that person permanently which very well may not be your intention or your desire.

Another danger is that casting any spell or conducting any ritual will reduce the intended target's ability to protect him or herself from negative energies. This makes the targeted individual more susceptible to other curses.

Yet another risk associated with casting love spells is that if done incorrectly, you could target the wrong person, thus causing them to fall in love with someone else or causing you to fall in love with the wrong person. Given the seriousness and long-term effects of these spells, you do not want to take the chance that the spell ends up impacting someone other than the intended target.

Finally, you should be very careful that if you do ever cast a love spell with the intention of drawing someone to you, you need to then treat that person with respect and kindness. If you cause someone to fall in love with you and then treat them badly, this could have a substantially negative impact on your own karma.

These potential consequences all provide an excellent reason why you should avoid carrying out love spells or rituals. The final reason is that many believe that love is one area where free will alone should come into play, and no artificial influence should determine who anyone should love.

Having said all of that, love spells and rituals are very common in the practice of Voodoo, and it is important that you understand and recognize them even if you have no intention of conducting them yourself. If you are able to see the signs of a love spell, you will be better equipped to avoid being the target of one yourself or having someone you know be a target and you will be better prepared to overcome any love spell that another practitioner may have cast.

Anointing Voodoo Oil

This recipe will make the target desire the spell-caster. First, select your carrier oil. Fill the bottle's cap, or another small vessel, with oil and place one of your eyelashes into the oil. Leave the mixture overnight. The next day, you will need to use your wiles to figure out how to get the target of your ritual to touch the oil with his or her index finger for a minute. Once the person has touched the oil, take their finger and brush it over your lips like you are putting on lipstick, but with the oil instead. Then kiss the individual with your lips closed.

There are obvious limitations to this ritual. First, you must have fairly close access to the target, in order to get him or her to touch the oil and allow you to kiss their fingers and their lips. This spell is best used on someone with whom you already have that kind of relationship, as a means of enhancing their feelings and commitment toward you.

Candlewax Cover

This spell will make the object of your affection more attracted to you. You will need a piece of paper, a purple and a red candle, and a shallow disposable pan. Purple is a blend of the colors blue and red, which represent the sky and blood respectively. This combination will take your target's affection and direct it toward your blood, i.e. your physical self.

Write the name of your target on the left side of the paper. You must write the name four time, because that is a number of power in Voodoo. Next, write your name on the right side of the paper five times. After you have written the names, light the candle and let four droplets of wax fall onto the left side of the paper where you have written your target's name. Then fold the paper in two so that your names touch his or hers – the wax will seal the names together.

Then put the paper into the pan and pour enough water over it so that the paper is covered. Set the red candle onto the paper and light the candle. Once all of the wax from the red candle has melted into the water, the object of your affection will similarly melt into your arms.

Return of a Lover

If your lover has left you and you wish to get him or her back, this spell is the one to use. Be cautioned, though: it is a very powerful spell and you must be absolutely certain that you are carrying it out exactly right.

Use some of your target's hair and clothing to make a Voodoo doll, as set out earlier in this book. Making the body out of the person's unwashed t-shirt will make the spell particularly powerful. If you are able to get different items of his or her clothing, use fragments of that clothing to make the doll's clothing for the corresponding part. For example, if you are able to get a t-shirt of and a pair of jeans, use a piece of the t-shirt to make the torso and a piece of the jeans to make the legs.

Once you have made the doll, pin it to the pillow in your bed where the person would lay if he or she were sleeping with you. Talk to the doll as though it were your target, focusing on your target while you speak. This will create a psychic connection with your target and will draw him or her back to you.

Bewitching Spell

This is another powerful spell, which should be used lightly or without serious consideration for the possible side effects. This ritual will make the target fall in love with you, so you should be very sure that this is what you want on a permanent basis – it may be difficult or even impossible to overturn the effects of the spell if you wish to do so at a later date.

To start the ritual, dedicate a Voodoo doll to your target so that it is connected to and represents him or her. While adding elements of the target like you usually would, also add elements from yourself – hair, nail clips, clothing you or your target have worn. When you have finished the doll, carve your beloved's name into the doll.

This spell must be performed on the day following the new moon. Prepare your altar as we have discussed earlier in this book, and light an appropriate candle. Take a ribbon in each of red, white, and black, and wrap the doll in each piece. You can knot the ribbons as necessary to ensure that they stay in place and attached to the doll. While you are wrapping the doll, recite the following incantation: "Ribbons bind and entwine your heart, linked to mine."

Once you have wrapped the doll in all three ribbons, write the name of your target on a piece of paper and leave that paper on your altar. Place the doll onto the piece of paper and snuff the candle.

The next night, go back to your altar. Re-light the candle and hold the doll in your hands, chanting the following: "For you I yearn; for me you burn." Place the doll onto the paper once more, but this time allow the candle to continue burning for at least one hour. Keep the doll on your altar until the effects of the spell come about and the object of your affection has fallen in love with you. Then wrap the doll in cloth and place it somewhere safe so that the attraction is guaranteed to continue.

Petitioning the Love Spirit to Help You

This spell is one of the safer love spells, because it is not meant to be targeted at a specific individual. Rather, it is intended as a mean of getting assistance from the love spirit (Erzulie Fréda) to help you find love; you will still find love through the usual, non-magical means, but your chances of doing so are greater with the assistance of the spirit.

To conduct this ritual, you will need the following ingredients:

- A pink candle
- Scissors
- Red or pink construction paper or cardboard
- A saucer or plate
- 2 cups of sugar
- 1 tbsp. of cinnamon
- 1 tbsp. of ginseng powder

Prepare the candle for the ritual by purifying and blessing it, as discussed in previous chapters of this book. Mix the ginseng powder, sugar, and cinnamon. Cut a Voodoo doll shape out of the construction paper or cardboard, and write your goals and desires on the back of the doll. Specific about *what* you are looking for but not *whom* you are looking for.

Once you have readied the doll, light the candle and call upon Erzulie Fréda. Repeat your requests out loud, speaking clearly and showing your intention to attract love as it is meant for you without improperly influencing any one individual to fall in love with you.

If you do wish to identify a specific person as the target of the spell, you can write their name on the doll's front thirteen times, then write your own name over each name. Be warned that this may actually make the spell less powerful, because the intention is to attract the person with whom you are meant to be, not for you to choose the person with whom you will be.

Whether you have written a specific person's name on the doll or not, place the doll on the saucer or cup and sprinkle the herb-sugar mixture over it. Then place the candle on the doll's middle, surrounded by the herb-sugar concoction, and once again state your wishes, concentrating on your goals.

Allow the candle to burn for thirteen minutes, while continuously repeating your desires. Be as honest and open as possible, so that Erzulie Fréda can see that you are operating with good intentions and in harmony with the universe.

After the thirteen minutes have passed, gather the dish, doll, herb-sugar mixture, and any wax drippings and place them together near or at your altar. Repeat the ritual each day for the next thirteen days. Then put the doll in a safe place and keep it there until your goals have come true.

It is vitally important that when you do find the person that you love, you thank Erzulie Fréda for her assistance; if you do not, she may get angry and intervene in your happiness. Return the Voodoo doll to the natural environment by burying it, burning it, or throwing it into a body of water.

Love Floor Wash

This is another love spell that is fairly safe to use because, like the spell above, it is generally focused on finding love rather than capturing the attention of one specific individual. The recipe for this spell involves the following ingredients:

- One quart of clean stream water or fresh rain water
- Half of a fresh lime
- Five drops of pure rose oil
- One bay leaf (whole)
- A few white mustard seeds (whole)

Mix all of the ingredients together and let the concoction steep for at least one hour. Then, on your hands and knees, wash your kitchen floor with the mixture. You do not need to scrub or put any particular effort into it, you just need to make sure that the whole floor is covered. As soon as the floor dries, it will start to draw love to you.

Chapter 10: Advanced Spells for Healing

Healing spells are one of the most positive type of spells that are practiced in Voodoo, and for the most part are very good for your karma. There are many different spells and rituals that can be used to heal yourself or others, whether you are healing physical, emotional, or mental harms.

Make It Well Spell

This is a simple Voodoo doll spell that you can use to heal yourself or others. The items that you will require are easily gathered: blue fabric, a couple of handfuls of dried beans (any type of bean), piece of white paper, and two small white buttons.

Cut up the fabric into two pieces that are shaped roughly like a person. Sew the exterior seam of most of the doll's body, leaving enough of a space to put in the beans. Draw a cross shape onto the paper, and put the paper into the doll with the beans. Sew the doll the rest of the way up, and fasten the two buttons where the eyes would be. Place the doll under your bed (or the bed of the person being healed), and keep there until the illness has passed.

Herbal Health

This spell is best used for healing yourself, although you can use it to heal others if you have access to some of their hair. To carry out this spell, you will need the following ingredients:

- White felt or fabric
- Needle, scissors, thread
- A piece of jade or hematite (or both is best)
- Some of fennel, rosemary, mint, bittersweet, St. John's Wort, angelica root
- Some strands of your hair
- Blue marker or pen

Use the white material to make a Voodoo doll, sewing the seams so that only a small hole is left for placing the stuffing. Wrap your hair around the jade or hematite and place that into the doll's head. Fill the remainder of the doll with whichever herbs you have selected from the list, and sew the doll shut. On the doll's chest, draw a circle, then draw a heart in the circle. This is a basic health charm that you can leave on your altar or another quiet spot until you have overcome whatever illness or harm you were suffering.

Light of Health

If you have a minor cold or twisted ankle, or some other injury that is not too serious but is inconvenient, this spell will help you to heal it. All that you will need is a white candle and something that you can use to carve images into the candle.

Carve the following runes into the side of the candle:

ᚾᛋᚠ

Each of these runes symbolizes success, good health, and energy. If there is room on the candle, carve each symbol several times. Place the candle onto your altar and then light it. While focusing on the flame, visualize its light flowing through you and giving you healing and good health. Allow the candle to burn out on its own.

Loco and Ghede Healing Spell

This spell involves petitioning the Loa Loco and Ghede. Ghede (also known as Papa Ghede) controls the eternal crossroads and is known as the spirit of death, but also of resurrection. Loco is the spirit of plants and is closely associated with trees. He has healing properties, and is the patron of holistic and herbal doctors. Loco's powers of healing and Ghede's powers of resurrection combine in this spell to assist with healing from more serious illnesses.

First you must start with a blank Voodoo doll – one that has not yet been made to represent any specific individual. To call Ghede and Loco, blow into the doll's mouth and nose areas. Then dedicate the doll to the person who is sick by calling that person's name three times and 'baptizing' the doll. The dedication will be most effective if you incorporate some of the person's hair or fingernails into the doll.

Once you have made the doll, visualize separating the disease from the patient, and transferring the disease to the doll. Once you have a strong visualization of this process, drive the nail into the doll at the location where the disease originated on the person. The nail will keep the disease in the doll so that it does not return to the person.

This spell is best conducted during a waning moon, and requires intensive concentration. Once you see that the spell has begun to work, place the doll in running water or bury it.

Rejuvenation Spell

This spell requires the participation of another person. You will need to recruit an assistant who is younger than you and of the same sex. The assistant must be friendly, full of energy, and willing to share the energy with you. Standing beside you, the assistant should hold your doll gently. Concentrate on your assistant's energy while he or she stands beside you. After 5 minutes, you will be rejuvenated. This spell will not hurt the assistant in any way.

Chapter 11: Other Useful Spells

Each of the chapters above have addressed spells that fall under certain categories, such as healing, love, protection, and revenge. There are many other kinds of Voodoo spells and rituals though, that do not necessarily fall under a larger category. This chapter will talk about some of those other spells, and teach you how to conduct the appropriate rituals.

Contacting the Dead

This spell will allow you to contact and communicate someone who is deceased. To carry out this spell, you will require the following ingredients:

- Incense sticks
- Black cloth
- Light red, scented candle
- Ivory candle
- Bowl of water
- Manuka oil

Place the incense sticks on the black cloth, in a triangle shape. Place the red candle inside the triangle, and light it with the flame from the ivory candle. Write the name of the deceased person on a piece of paper. Place the bowl of water inside the triangle with the red candle.

Rub the Manuka oil onto the paper with the person's name, and burn the paper with the ivory candle. Take the ashes from the paper and mix them into the water, reciting an incantation wherein you ask the life beyond life to come forward as you call, and to speak through the water as you speak through the mirror. The exact words are not important, as long as the basic concept is communicated.

Once you have said the incantation, the spirit of the deceased person should appear like a reflection in the water. If the water shakes then the spell is working; if not, you may need to repeat the incantation a few more times. Eventually, you will be able to communicate with the deceased person through their reflection in the water.

Summoning a Spirit

Unlike the spell above, this spell will summon an actual spirit, not a deceased person. This is an important difference. To perform this spell you will need to gather the following items:

- Round red cloth
- Goat hair
- Black candles

- Purple, cinnamon-scented candles

This spell must be performed in a location where you are able to see the footprints that you leave behind when you walk. On a beach in the sand is an excellent location, for example. It must also be performed on a night where there is a new moon, as this is when the spirits are strongest and can easily be summoned.

Draw a circle in the sand, fifty centimeters in diameter. Place the red cloth in the circle. The red cloth does not need to be the same size as the drawn circle – it can be smaller, but it should not be bigger. Place the goat hair onto the red cloth.

Place the black and purple candles around the cloth, and light the candles. Walk around the cloth four times (it does not matter in which direction you walk), making sure that all of your footprints can be seen. Once you have completed the fourth circle raise your hands into the air, close your eyes, and recite an incantation where you are calling beyond life to bring the deceased back to the land of the living. Ask the deceased to follow your footsteps back through the sand. As with the spells above, the exact words of the incantation are less important than the message being communicated.

As you can see, it is important that your footsteps can be seen so that the spirit is able to follow them to reach you. Remember that spirits can be quite strong, so you must concentrate very hard on the spell and do not show any fear. When you want to banish the spirit back to its plane, state the following: "As I repeat this new verse, I undo this holy curse."

Knot Spell

This spell is a basic and straight-forward spell that will help you to get rid of your problems. Select a piece of yarn in a color that is appropriate to your problem – e.g. red for love, green for money. While holding the yarn in your hands, pour out all of your problems and frustrations. Then tie the yarn into knots, symbolizing that you feel tied up. Take the yarn outside and let it blow away in the wind along with your problems. To finish up the spell, take a cleansing ritual shower or bath. This spirit is best done during the full moon.

Banishing Barriers

This spell will help you to identify and remove obstacles that are preventing you from succeeding in some area of your life. Whether it is a love crisis or a problem at work, this spell can get the obstacle out of your way. While the spell is generally focused at all of the Voodoo gods, you may wish to focus on Chango in particular. Chango is the spirit of fire, thunder, and lightning.

To perform this spell, you will need:

- Four whole hot chili peppers
- Small fragment of broken glass
- Dark rum
- Ceramic bowl, black

State your obstacle or barrier loudly and clearly, and ask the gods to remove the barrier. Place the glass into the bottom of the bowl then put the peppers in on top of the glass. Once again make the request for the obstacle to be removed, loudly and clearly. Pour the rum into the bowl so that the peppers are covered, and take a small drink for yourself.

Place the bowl under a tree outside your home – the bigger that the tree is, the more effective the spell will be. The next morning, pour the contents of the bowl out onto the Earth.

Good Luck Floor Wash

This is a general spell that will help to bring good luck and fortune into your home. All that will you need is

Van Van oil and a bucket of clean, warm water. Add two tablespoons of the oil to the bucket of water – exact measurements are not important. You should be able to faintly smell the oil when you have mixed it with the water.

Using a sponge or mop, wipe down a room in your house that is busy, such as the living room or kitchen. Do not allow anyone to walk in the area until it has dried thoroughly. Within seven days, you should experience some good fortune.

Paper Money Spell

This is another spell that will help to bring you some good luck, this time in the form of bringing you some money. You will need to gather the following things:

- Red thread and needle
- One piece of paper money
- One piece of red cloth that is bigger than the paper money
- At least one cup of coarse salt
- Orange oil
- Pink candles
- Amber incense

Using the needle and thread, gently sew the paper money onto the cloth. Hang the cloth on the wall over your altar or a table, so that you are able to spread the rest of the ingredients out below it.

On the altar or table, pour the salt in thick lines to make a square. Place a candle at each corner of the square, and light the candles. Put an open dish of orange oil in the middle of the square. Dip your incense stick into the oil and then light it in a holder that is outside of the square. Say the following words out loud: "Pinned to my life evermore, go with me to every shore. I trade you for another thing, come back to my pockets bring." (*Reference.com*)

Allow the candles and incense to burn for one hour, then blow them out. Leave all of the items set up, so that you can repeat the entire spell again at the same time of day for the next two days. You should receive some extra money within fifteen days.

Losing Weight Spell

There are Voodoo spells that can help you to change your looks in various ways. This spell, in particular, can assist you with losing weight. You will need four light-colored candles – two white, one light blue or purple, and one gold. The white candles will fill you with positive energy, the blue or purple will help your mind to focus on and understand what you are doing, and the gold candle will fill you with the powers of creation and health.

Place the four candles onto a table, in a generally circular shape. Light the candles and place your Voodoo doll in the middle of the circle. Undress the doll and place your finger on the area where you would like to lose the fat. Concentrate until you feel that part of your body warming up. Slowly press down and smooth your finger along the doll's body, smoothing away the fat. Focus on your body and smoothing the fat away from it at the same time.

If at any time during this ritual you do not feel well, immediately stop. Undress the doll, remove any hair from its head, and state that you are breaking the connection with it and that it is just a doll. Spit in the doll's face three times, and put out the candles. You should feel better within a couple of minutes.

Trust Spell

This spell is an effective way to increase the trust between any two people – spouses, lovers, business associates, or friends. To carry out this spell, you will need the following ingredients:

- Crushed sun-dried tomatoes
- Uncooked rice
- Powdered cinnamon
- Crushed cardamom seeds

The uncooked rice represents a situation that is binding for both parties. The tomatoes symbolize a good sex life (for romantic partners) or generally a healthy trust between two people. The cinnamon represents good communication, while the cardamom symbolizes loyalty. (*Wishbonix*) The exact portions of each ingredient are not important, as long as they are generally in equal proportions.

Mix the ingredients together in a bowl or other vessel, and scatter the concoction across a pathway that the other individual walks regularly.

The benefit of this spell is that it will cause the other person to trust you, so that you have a better chance of working through any problems that you may be experiencing.

Conclusion

Voodoo is one of the most intensely mystical religions that can ever be followed, if only because the sense of history looming over you crashes down in every 3000-year old rhythm passed through generations of high priests playing in a ritual gathering, with the beats and percussions of the instrument pounding along with the tempo of your very soul. However, beyond its *magical* aspects, as more concentrated upon in American Voodoo, this religion is also remarkable for its feeling of community and the sense of belonging from its practitioners, no matter which corner of the world you travel to. It's largely because of that fact that the immense complexity of this spiritual system can't be transmitted solely through literary offerings in its name, and requires first hand experiential dealings in order to eke out their complete measure.

So, just as I once found myself walking down this path, I hope you find your feet dragging you towards a worthy Houngan or Mambo who will initiate you to its many mysteries, as well as help you cope with the tremendous effects these revelations will have upon your personality and your perspective on the world around you. But, if they bring up mentions of financial requirements to take you under their wing—scram in the opposite direction.

In the end, remember this—you can't choose your patron spirits, beyond a few that would help if you request earnestly enough. With some others, trying to persuade them to help you when they seem silent may simply result in mischief on their part, which may not go so well for you. Stay away from love potions and spells—the heart is part of magic so ancient that no one can entirely understand its interactions. Therefore, if you try to force someone to be yours when it's not meant to be, you'll be destroying the lives of many more than just the other person—you'll also be interfering with your own happiness, as well as that of the person who would have otherwise made you happy, and the person who would have been happy with the person whom you cast your spell upon.

Similarly, stay away from revenge spells and other such negative magic. It's often said that those who wish to dig someone else's grave should prepare two in advance, one for their target as well as one for themselves. And nowhere does that hold more true than in Voodoo, where every action has amplified consequences. May the Lwa watch over you, but not *too* closely. May Papa Legba always answer your call.

Finally, I'd like to thank you for purchasing this book! If you enjoyed it or found it helpful, I'd greatly appreciate it if you'd take a moment to leave a review on Amazon. Thank you!

Printed in Great Britain
by Amazon